reveals of the Soul

L. N Wyman

reveals of the Soul

L. N Wyman

"may your own truths
be found in your own journey"

L. N. Wyman

contents

reveals of the soul

last time I checked
my hands
as well as yours
are full of the sins we committed
I don't believe either of us
have room to hold stones

We both live in glass homes

Why must I fear the storm?
for without it
I would not have known
how strong this vessel was

ships are not used to sail rivers,
yet, are boats.
But ships,
ships are used to sail vast oceans

I cannot fear the storm
for it was sent
to make me wise
to make me strong
to make   me

to mold me
into the vessel
I was meant to be

There is no swifter executioner
to dreams than the   wait
                    for validation.
Believe in it yourself.
For every good and perfect gift
comes from the father of lights.

you have all you need.

love yourself enough to be
honest

with yourself.

that is the first step to killing
the fear
disguised as practicality
in your life.

what you want isn't impossible

just know
you can fail
at what you don't want
just the same.

If we knew
how dangerous it is
to give up too soon

Because I, too
have felt the pain
of holding on.

but,

if words could retract in time
back to places we couldn't
places only love could reach

I'd tell you

it's worth it

these things of men
will never make me

Both of us
beggars
in search
of food veiled as life
I wish to only show you
where my bread comes from

"Speak
to those demons
like you know
who you are"

Gospels,
Nothing
short of promises

sung in the tune of
"things get better"

I need them.

She is done.
It doesn't mean
she doesn't love you.
It doesn't mean
she does not care.
It doesn't mean
she does not wish things were different,
that you didn't mess up,
that she wasn't so stuck in her beliefs,
that she doesn't wish to take you back.

It just means she is done.

But the reasons why I am done,
it is not because
i cannot wait,
it is not because,
i have moved on,
it is not because,
my feelings have moved me to feel different.
It is not because
i have fallen out of love.

It's actually the contrast,
i have fallen deeper,

but not just with you
with the Man who created you.
With myself.
With where I am now,
and I cannot be around anything
that pulls me away
from truths such as those.

truths

O, time
why
must it always feel
like you betray
those who need you most.

Emotions
how you betray us.
You rise and fall
as the tides of the sea

I've learned to be moved
by principles and promises

Not just any principles, but
God's principles
for his ways
always seem to be out of our grasp

Not just any promises, but
God's promises
for his words
have shown to be
ever-present, and everlasting

I refuse to dim the light placed
deep within me
to allow yours to shine
where it is not meant to be

your light is just as bright,
you just so happen to be
shining it in the wrong places

reveals of the soul

this body is built on
Everlasting Promises

not reflections of yourself.

keep your opinions
I do not need them

so many men
following creeds of men
not knowing they are
flying together.

Cicadas.

unaware of the blind leading the blind.

if you plan to do it
do it.
do not be subtle.

for the human mind does not accept subtle
when posed against what it knows best

with the strength of a thousand men
I put my war clothes on for battle.

Armor and Sword
in hand

The reign of these demons
will be decided here and now,

and I have no intention on
losing.

you refuse to treat me
as the man I am now
and i guess
rightfully so

but I have no room
for those who cannot see,
those who cannot appreciate
the man filling these shoes

for these shoes
have many steps to go
and cannot afford to carry
dead weight

May your best years be before you
May your dreams be closer than arms reach
you deserve it
May you continue to travel
for more people need to be touched
for more people need to see
a woman like you
May your faith grow stronger
so that you may have strength
to do what you have been called
May you have more joy
and more life

Happy Birthday

*text
never
sent*

the difference between
who i am now

and

who I am destined to be
relies solely in
the application of
the 24 hours
i've been given
just like everyone else.

wish i knew that Tuesday
before i ate those damn churros

late
night
revelations

whenever   vulnerable
i feed my spirit first and foremost
for it is fire
that fuels
this body of
flesh and dreams

i never told Him
that i didn't need you

maybe that's why I'm
doing just fine.

Still remember
saying to myself
"Look at him giving his life to the lord,
That's Good."
The type of "Good" that's
"good for you" good, but not
"good for me" good

The type of "Good" said from a distance
because you have to give up too much to be
that "Good"

I'm sure someone
right now
is looking at me
saying the same thing

Trust me
you are already worthy
of being that good.

reveals of the soul

that
"Good"

i wish to be fearless
in one thing,
wearing
the badge
that says
I belong to you

They say
misery loves company
but i disagree
for when i am low,
with all my might
i brighten the room around me
for i never
would want someone
to be near the feeling

i do not want any company

I remember saying
"I hope she doesn't fall in love
with a painter"
Who wouldn't want to be painted
as they slept?

then she left

which left me
finding ways to paint emotions
with words that speak
long after your footsteps left

I, too,
became a painter of the sorts
now creating hope
out of painful memories
that were necessary.

fuck
Artists

her skin,
be like gold
Pure.
like how we
once were.

look at her
both
magic and prose
the only way
they can be coupled

outside of fiction

i've felt pain
that made me
work muscles
i have forgotten about.
i know this
because i am here.
Survived

Makes me wonder
what is this "thing"
that you have called me
to survive for?

I see.

Purpose.
the cure
for survivor's remorse.

the
cure

O
the stories battered flesh
would sing
if death
were to be held at bay
if only just for   a moment.
And if those silenced voices
were sure to be set free,

I'm sure there would
be nothing but a choir
of Untold Truths
taken to the

grave.

dead men tell no tales

Flesh,

        where I am going,
you,   you cannot come.

reveals of the soul

I found out that
words;
raise spirits from the dead,
tear new rooms in closed minds,
mold broken pieces of hearts
back together with gold
can make...

i needed to hear no more
to realize what
i planned to do
with them.

I've been broken
but I've found what i was made of
I love it
I have not any money
For now i know what to do with it
when i get it
i've learned.
I've been so low,
I'm thankful
for now I know how
to reach heights that
no man can take away

and the best part

I know how to bring others with me

for my
good

"You're always going to be missing out
on something child.
I know your every thought.
Finding out what's worth
missing out on,
now that,
that, my child,
is the secret
to time"

"I had to break you"

"But why? I thought you loved me"

"I had to make sure you knew,
 it was not your gifts,
 but grace that brought you
 where this promise is".

and the boy said
"where are we going?"
and He responded
"Do I not know all?
Am I not all?
Do I not love you?
Trust me, I will do
what you ask of me
as long as you handle
what I ask of you"

dialogues with God

the one who sows,
the one who eats,

both have their burdens

And they
have gotten through worse
with faith

We are no different.

The woman who loves hard
there is nothing stronger
nor, more beautiful.
Except for the woman
who loves God
more than herself.
For she
can love
past her breaking point
over
and over
and over again

reflection of God

I am
the summation
of all things prayed for.
I am the results of
bruised knee caps
from a mother and father's
dialogue with God.
Your words will never
destroy me.

Armor

why is it that beautiful things
come with beautiful burdens

I find this
to be true,
but so is this,

that they always come
with blessings
that outweigh them.

David says
"I do not wish to engage in battle without God"

So before my enemy is slain,
my knees draw first blood.

even the most unholy of wounds
will eventually feel like
trivial
necessary
knee scrapes
that help you learn
like you never failed
and love like you were never hurt

But only
and only
in the presence of God.

Carefully aimed.
Patiently waited
for the perfect
opportunity
to hit head on

the enemy took
his best shot.
my spirit
still unbroken.

that's when I realized
I serve a God who lets
rogue bullets hit
only...
if he wants,
to give me a reminder
of how strong he built this soul.

Hey,
wanted to let you know I'm leaving soon.
You still have ample time to think.
No pressure.
I didn't call to talk about that,
but I want you to know that
I am dedicated and committed to being
in communication with you
Even if I'm away.
You said it yourself, "You make time
for what's what's worth it"
and my heart is still with you
no matter where my body is present.

I plan on coming back twice a month to
visit my pops. Buying my tickets out ahead of
time as soon as I get my schedule.

I don't know what you necessarily need
in terms of time or space,
and I may not know
any of those, but I am willing to be patient.

But I want to know who you are now,
if your dreams are still the same,
what you believe in,
what excites you,
if the left side of your
face is still your favourite side.
If your smile is still the same.
Not just any smile, but the smile when your gums
show and the corners of your eyes squint up

And you don't have to answer this now.
Take as much time as God allows

No distance is too far
If it is for you,
I know it will be worth it.

the
before

i can count
how many times
her ghost sat next to me.
The same amount of times
I wished i didn't have to.

neither of us are the same
but so are butterflies who have grown
into beautiful things,
remnants of who they once were.
Molded by the journey
Molded into something beautiful
that could never have become
without the closed circumstances
that birthed it

So many things we learn in retrospect.
To think what we could save

if we believed
the dots connected
before they did.

Let these Good wounds
make you strong.

My worth is not
dictated by your wants.

"I love you
but you will not destroy me"

remembering that moment in the car
dropping you off
and i said
"Hey, lets do it"

And you thought i would say no
you couldn't believe it

I still remember that day
because I am thankful for it.

We search for those next moments of
joy
excitement
fire
to escape everyday life.

the monotony.

it's not like it comes to and end.

it's just when you found the right person
they just so happen
to make every moment
of monotony
damn good

stuck in between the seams
neither fabric, nor thread
but mixtures of both
all simultaneously filled with hope
and despair.

tomorrow will take care of itself
but today, we
control this moment

i missed her
and telling her
to wear jeans with heels

I was upset
at the time
you were placed in my life

The reuniting
of two
made separate in
flesh
but whole
 in spirit

The full expression of man

the First Marriage

Daughter of the Divine,
the pieces that make you
need to be cherished.

I know where you come from.

this love will never change
even when the flowers wilt
when wrinkles take hold
when the leaves' pigment gives out

it will stay
and it will outlive us

i saw myself looking through the eyes of Daniel
asking him to show me what he saw
when the rusted chains wouldn't shatter,
when those beasts encircled him,
"How could you sleep?"

Never did I see
what happened between
that moment of
swallowing fear
and
perfect peace.

"What does this faith look like?"
He's told me this, but what does it look like
to believe?

I see.

He slept because he saw the word,
the speech,
the promise,
of God
like words manifested into comfort.

I see.

To tell someone how the storm ends
in the standing of its eye,
is where lore is replaced with
faith.

The in-between of "what is" and "what is to come"
is where You create the literal manifestation
of faith.

Its something i can hold.
It is different from my speech,
but it's a shadow of the same process.
This must be so if I am made
in Your essence.
i may speak things so that they may exist,
but as You, when You speak, it exists.
I,
am only similar.

for You
speech doesn't ensue
creation,
it is,
as it is spoken.

I see.

my speech is only like   Yours.

Speech

Some of us
are attempting to save those
who don't believe they are in need of saving.
I find it best to pray that love lights their way.
There will be a time when the strength
of the human will, will betray,
and that is when love lights the blackened path
that appears when the next step is veiled.

Love is not bitter.
Love is not prideful.
Love is not selfish.

Sometimes people
have to find their own way.
Because it is never
real love, Godly love,
until people have the choice
to decide
for themselves.

It hurts to desire
and not have.
Most people can't do it.

To want something so
and be posed against
the idea of not having it.

But that's where most people fail.
The courage to be honest
with the desires one wants,
together
with the tenacity to patiently,
wait

Gives the strength to thrive
no matter the outcome.
Whichever way it goes.

we may have only had a few
conversations
but i can only imagine the woman
that you are fully
for being in contact with your beautiful
and amazing daughter
she is a true testament of beauty from the inside
out
she has truly been made in the image of
our creator
and I thank God for that
but I thank God for you as well because
you have raised that woman and she is
shadow of you and your faith

So thank you

Happy Mother's day

Delivery Status Notification (Failure)

Pain
the way it teaches,
it is the most unforgiving,
yet boundlessly rewarding.
It is the most painful,
yet, it births a plethora of new
in the graveyards of old comfort.
It is bitter,
but yet, it gives abundance
out of necessary grit.
Each story begins with a start,
whether good or bad,
that is up you,
but it starts
the moment you accept
that you are the author of your life.
so write
and live
your best story

letter from the Author

your
beginning